Your First
PARROT

Martin Gabin

t.f.h.
Your First
PARROT
Martin Gabin

CONTENTS

Pages 2-3
and 34-35:
Photos by
Robert Pearcy

© 1991
By T.F.H.
Publications,
Inc., Neptune,
N.J. 07753 USA

•

T.F.H.
Publications,
The Spinney,
Parklands,
Denmead,
Portsmouth
PO7 6AR
England

History

All parrots and parrot-type birds have been popular pets through the ages. The Asiatic parakeets were brought into Europe during the time of Alexander the Great. Indeed the Alexandrine parakeet derives its name from this potentate.

In other periods of history, other parrots have come to the attention of the civilized world. Sailors and travellers to Africa, Asia, and the Americas brought back various members of the parrot family from their travels. Later the Australian cockatoos, parakeets, and lorikeets were brought back and quickly achieved popularity. So you see the popularity of parrot-type birds is by no means a phenomenon of our current century. These attractive birds have been popular down through the centuries.

The United States was the natural habitat of only one parrot-type bird, the Carolina parakeet. This bird was wantonly destroyed by the thousands for its plumage and as a consequence is now extinct.

Parrot-type birds are commonly reputed to live to a great old age. Although many of them do live to be fifty years old or more, stories of parrots living to be seventy-five or a hundred should be taken with a grain of salt. An occasional bird may achieve such great age, but only very rarely.

Considering the potential long life of a parrot, paying a high price is certainly justified, as the care and feeding of the bird are not particularly expensive. Historically, caged birds were kept by the aristocracy. The lower classes did not discover the charms of caged birds until the Industrial Revolution.

Additionally, the longevity of a parrot should jog the conscience of potential keepers—unlike a goldfish that may expire within a year or two, a properly kept parrot is a long-term commitment of time, energy, and finance.

Alexandrine parrot.

Why a Parrot?

I know of no more satisfying or rewarding pet than a tame and intelligent bird of the parrot family. With their ability to mimic the human voice and their comical ways, they furnish an endless source of amusement for their owners and friends. They can also bring about some awfully embarrassing situations!

I remember one occasion several years ago in a pet shop when a grade school teacher brought her class of thirty children to see the birds and animals that were on sale there. The children were everywhere and into everything and pandemonium ruled! When the confusion was at its height, a huge scarlet macaw added her voice to the general bedlam. In order to quiet her, the owner of the shop took the bird out of her cage and put her on her wrist. A few minutes later, the teacher lined the children up to leave. As the last child marched out of the door the teacher said, "Thank you so much, I hope we haven't been too much trouble." The shop owner replied, "Not at all." About this time the macaw shrieked in unmistakable syllables, "Oh, Yeah! Haw-haw-haw-haw."

They say that parrots can't think but only mimic familiar sounds. I sometimes wonder.

Some parrots are quite friendly with everybody and some are "one-man birds." Most have distinct likes and dislikes, being quite fond of some people and antagonistic to others. Some like men and dislike women, others the reverse. As a general rule, a female bird will become more attached to men and a male bird, more attached to women. They are all rather temperamental and unpredictable birds, and there is no accounting for some of their actions. As a rule, if they have good care and the proper diet, they become quite docile and their amusing ways soon make them a real part of the family.

It is my purpose to tell you how to give your parrot the proper amount of care and training it requires so that your pet will be a source of satisfaction and amusement to you for many, many years. Again I remind you that proper training is paramount to years of pleasure and companionship.

The care and the training that you give your bird is of immense importance. The joy that you get from your parrot can only be measured by the amount of care and training you give to it. If it is not healthy or if you do not have its trust and confidence, you cannot expect your parrot to be a docile and affectionate pet. The time and effort you put into its care and training will pay rich dividends in the future.

Above: A real parrot's parrot—the Amazon parrot is the choice of many psittacine lovers. This blue-fronted Amazon enjoys a treat. Photo by Isabelle Francais. **Opposite:** The largest family members, the macaws are brilliantly colored parrots that can make affectionate, attentive pets when reared from youth. Scarlet and blue and gold macaws photographed by Michael De Freitas.

Which One?

What is a parrot? Walking into your local pet shop and congenially assailing the proprietor with your enthusiasm to purchase a "parrot" can be a little risky. So, before you do so, consider that a parrot is a kind of bird, as opposed to a specific bird. From the majestic green-winged macaw to the exquisite purple-crowned lorikeet, parrot-like birds vary tremendously in size, type, required care, availability and subsequent cost. The aforementioned macaw, for instance, measures a length of 90 centimeters, while the tiny lorikeet, only 15 centimeters. The order of parrots is known as Psittaciformes and all members of this order share similar characteristics. For instance, no matter what size, color, or continent of origin, all parrots have hooked bills, tongues that are mallet-shaped, harsh voices, powerful legs, and the ability to mimic.

The birds are divided up many times into smaller, more specific groups—the most specific of these are species and subspecies. All members of a species look similar and can produce like-looking progeny. The differences from one subspecies to the next may be geography, size, and/or color patterns.

POPULAR PARROTS

No pet shop or aviary could possibly offer every kind of parrot; many parrots are very rare, even within their original habitats—such birds are called endangered. Other parrots have been bred in captivity with success and are more accessible to the public. Depending on the kind of parrot you want, the cost will vary greatly. Learn as much as you can about the parrot species you like before attempting to purchase it.

It is not possible to list every species and subspecies of parrot in the world in a book this size. Following is a compilation of some of the parrots which have become popular within the pet world. A potential owner may even find some of these birds difficult to locate, but proper connections and patience are the key to success in this area.

For the sake of our discussion, we can divide the parrot family into two generic groups: the parakeets and the parrots. To understand the distinction between the two labels, you might consider the general rule that a parrot has a short tail, while a parakeet has a long tail. The budgerigar (called *the* parakeet in the United States) is aptly described as a parakeet because of its long tail. The budgie, as he is called affectionately the bird world over, presides as the most popular of all the parrot-family birds.

Parakeets: Let us discuss parakeets beyond the little budgie and make continental distinctions between them. There are three continents to consider: Asia, Australia and South America.

Asian Parakeets: These parakeets originate in the Indian subcontinent and nearby countries. Approximately 35 species and subspecies populate this group which is noted for their long tails and ringed necks. The Asian parakeets vary in availability and plenitude. The largest of the Asian parakeets is the Alexandrine parakeet or ringneck. These birds measure approximately 53 centimeters and therefore need a goodly amount of flying space. Alexandrines tend to breed more consistently than many of their ringnecked cousins.

The Indian ringneck or Bengal parakeet is another promising member of this group. These birds can be kept singly and are a popular option for parakeet keepers. Nearly 40 centimeters in length, it is the most widely bred of all parakeets and proves to be hardy and easy to acclimatize.

Some other Asian parakeets are the derbian parakeet, malabar parakeet, moustached parakeet and plum-headed parakeet. While equally as attractive as the Indian and Alexandrine parakeets, these birds are less easily bred and less commonly kept.

Australian Parakeets: These richly colored Aussies are a vigorous lot which breed prolifically under optimum circumstances. The group can be subdivided into three categories: grass parakeets, rosellas or broadtails, and "others." The grass parakeets are conveniently sized, beautifully plumaged birds which have proven good breeders in captivity. These attributes and charms have well benefited their popularity in the bird world. Grass parakeets epitomize the ideal aviary bird and the various species require very like management. Examples of grass parakeets include the blue-winged grass parakeet, elegant grass parakeet, Bourke's parakeet, splendid grass parakeet, and turquoisine grass parakeet. In size these birds range from 20 to 23 centimeters in length and the predominant color is green or olive green. Different species have identifying other-than-green-colored markings, such as chestnut shoulders, scarlet chests, blue wings, etc.

Rosellas, the second grouping of the Australian parakeets, exhibit a characteristic broadtail; indeed, they are sometimes referred to as "broadtails." Averaging 32 centimeters in length, rosellas are good-looking and relatively easy to acquire from pet dealers. Rosellas are not recommended for bird enthusiasts without prior breeding experiences. Among the rosellas most accessible and popular are the Adelaide rosella, Barnard's parakeet, common rosella, crimson rosella, golden-mantled rosella, mealy

Above: The yellow rosella is a commonly kept Australian parakeet. Rosellas are medium-sized parrots that present few problems with feeding or breeding. Photo by P. Leysen. **Opposite:** Another handsome Australian parakeet is the cockatiel. These sprightly and beautifully hued birds are ideal as single pets and are amenable to training. Photo by Isabelle Francais.

rosella, and western rosella. Spangled mantles grace the rosellas, excepting the Barnard's, and is, along with the broad tail, a hallmark of the species.

In the "other" category of Australian parakeets, we include the cockatiel, king parakeet, Princess Alexandra parakeet, red-rumped parakeet and rock pebbler parakeet.

The increasingly popular cockatiel is a top-notch choice for the new parakeet keeper, whether or not he plans to breed his birds. The cockatiel is an ideal single pet and is most biddable. Many owners have had excellent success with teaching the bird a few words and phrases. The color possibilities and overall appearance of the species are stunning and their popularity can be attributed to any and all of these positive pet traits.

The red-rumped parakeet remains a popular choice among parrot keepers who are delighted by its colorful plumage, ease of breeding, and general hardiness. These parakeets are notably gregarious and will tolerate any of a number of birds in their aviary, including finches, cockatiels and other parakeets.

South American Parakeets: The parakeets in this flock do not originate solely in South America, but also in Central America and Mexico as well. This group can be subdivided into two: conures and conurine parakeets.

Conures vary in their popularity and have a distinctive look about

them. The conure's head and beak are exceptionally large, while the body is thin and the tail tapers. In size conures exhibit great variation, ranging from 23 to 53 centimeters in length. Although the conure does not generally breed profusely in captivity, it is an easy bird to care for and feed, proving to be a hardy, adaptable pet. Overall green predominates, but splashes of white, orange, red, yellow, and/or blue liven up the plumages.

Geography has notably affected the various conures. From Panama we meet the brown-eared conure; from Brazil, the golden-crowned conure; from Argentina, the Pantagonian conure; from South America, Quaker's conure. Other popular conures include Petz's conure, the nanday conure, the jenday conure, Queen of Bavaria conure, the white-eared conure and the red-bellied conure.

Conurine parakeets in this group are smallish and are generally considered close relatives to conures. Sweet and peace-loving in nature, the 16 or more species bunched under this parakeet umbrella are popular pets, despite their somewhat dull coloration. Most owners have good experience with keeping conurine parakeets singly, although pairs are evidently favored by fanciers, due to their moderate size. Among the conurine parakeets are the bee bee parakeet, canary-winged parakeet, tui parakeet, and white-winged parakeet. These prove to be the most accessible of the domesticated conurine parakeets.

Parrots: The more daring and adventurous of parrot enthusiasts who is looking for a larger, more dramatic-appearing bird must look to the second group, which we refer to as "parrots and parrot-like species." This is not to suggest that the aforementioned parakeets are not parrots, they indeed are; generally, though, they have longer tails.

When one hears the term parrot, he likely thinks of the first birds in this group, the African grey parrot and the Amazon parrot.

African Grey Parrot: Sometimes called the grey parrot, this parrot makes the best pet of all the large parrots. Notably affectionate and intelligent, the African grey is a good mimicker, with astonishing ability. Taming and training is best undertaken when the bird is still young, as adults can be more willful and difficult to break. In length, the grey parrot is 33 centimeters long. The adult plumage is a pale gray, marked with lighter and darker shades of gray and black on the body. The principle diet consists of seeds, nuts, and fruits. The demand for the grey parrot continues to peak in the pet world, as this bird has proven to be the best talker and more intelligent than the Amazon parrot. It is very difficult, however, to coerce the grey to speak on command.

Amazon Parrots: Amazons were once widely distributed across the South American continent, the only continent on which they naturally occur. All Amazons belong to the genus *Amazona*, which is divided into about 27 species. Some of the great Amazons are extinct today and many exist solely on one island, such as the St. Lucia or Puerto Rico Amazon. Medium in size, Amazons range from 25 to 36 centimeters and are principally green in coloration. Their tails are slightly rounded and their wings are round and broad. In addition to their superior talking abilities, they are also proficient, even acrobatic, climbers. Amazons are subject to whims and fleeting moments of bad temperament; like the African grey, the Amazon has a powerful screech which it uses with more or less discretion.

Among the more popular of the Amazons are the blue-fronted, festive, mealy, red-fronted, double yellow-headed, and yellow-fronted. The blue-fronted and festive are perhaps the most commonly kept Amazons.

There are other parrots, neither greys or Amazons, that should be counted here. The grand eclectus parrot, Maximillian's parrot, yellow-bellied Senegal parrot and the vernal hanging parrot are each notable and pleasant parrots that are kept in captivity. The least commonly kept of these is the grand eclectus which is an expensive and unfortunately scarce bird. Like the other parrots mentioned, this bird is highly attractive and colorful and quite amenable to life in captivity.

Cockatoos: Native to Australia and islands of the South Pacific, the

Above: The conures come from South America and have harsher voices than the Asian and Australian parakeets. The maroon-bellied conure is more broadly kept than many other conures. **Opposite:** One of the most trainable of all parrots is the African grey, revered as the best talker in the order. Photos by Isabelle Francais.

cockatoo is unique for its expressive head crest. The color is mostly white, sometimes with grayish shades throughout. A few cockatoos are black or gray. Size varies from 30 to 76 centimeters. Cockatoos are supreme entertainers, clown-like or dancer-like in their amusing often musical antics. These are long-lived, intelligent birds which are strong of body and voice. Ideally cockatoos are kept in aviaries since they are very active and, therefore, need room in which to exercise.

Of the cockatoo species, the umbrella cockatoo is among the most plentiful; it is found originally on the islands located northwest of New Guinea. The umbrella cockatoo is a large white cockatoo with yellow suffusion under the wings and tail. Some purport that cockatoos in general are not good eaters, and the umbrella supports this claim. Sunflower seeds, apples and corn on the cob are among this bird's more favored foods.

Considered the aristocrat of the genus, the greater sulphur-crested cockatoo can be as long as 56 centimeters and is truly splendid in its plumage. This bird is unmistakable in its dignity and stunning appearance.

Goffin's cockatoo is among the smallest of the genus, measuring only 30 centimeters in length. Its importation to the United States is a fairly recent occurrence. Popularity in the pet world is attributed to its convenient size, its appealing looks, and its pleasant disposition.

Another smallish cockatoo is the red-vented, also known as the Philippine cockatoo. These are clean, pleasant pets that surely delight their keen owners with their charming demonstrations of intelligence and play.

Lories: The subfamily known as Loriinae contains lories and lorikeets and closely related parrots such as lorilets and fig parrots. These are attractive, brilliantly colored parrots whose characteristic diet centers on fruit and nectar. It is the group's peculiar brush-like tongue that enables it to lap up nectar in a feline-like way. Lories are not generally considered easykeep parrots and should not be taken on by beginners. They make pleasant pets—it would seem that the lory finds captivity amenable to its tastes.

These birds are not seed-eaters like most other parrots, in fact the birds survive on a chiefly liquid diet: nectar syrup, honey, and evaporated milk. Fresh food must be provided *daily* without exception. Since the lory has difficulty keeping itself tidy in a confined space, providing the birds with as much room as possible is recommended.

Lories and lorikeets are delightful keepers, highly comical and amusing to watch. While these parrots enjoy the company of conspecifics, they tend to be "gang-oriented" and may assault another unexpected bird kept in the same cage. Generally speaking, lories are not recommended for beginning parrot keepers. At one time, when its feeding habits were less understood, the lory was considered a specialist's bird. Today, while it is true that lories require more experience and daily attentive care than other parrots, they are as long-lived, intelligent and enjoyable. The inexperienced bird keeper must be alerted to the lory's powerful bite, therefore proper handling is of particular importance. While any rightly kept lory can be a delight for its owner, the birds are generally deemed unpredictable and excitable. Novices are discouraged from obtaining a lory until they are somewhat experienced in birds or parrots.

Macaws: The mammoth macaw is the largest member of the parrot family, ranging in size from 36 to 91 centimeters. This latter measurement belongs to the exquisite hyacinth macaw, a dazzling blue chap, comparable in appearance and intelligence to any of the 24 species of the macaw genus *Ara*. The plumage of the macaw is undeniably brilliant, ranging in color from the deep lush blue of the hyacinth macaw to the sparkling red of the scarlet macaw. The characteristics of the genus include the large pointed beak, the pointed and lengthy tails, full plumage and a bald cheek patch on the face.

New owners are not inclined towards macaws, and rightly so. Macaws are not the choice of everyone. Even barring the high price tag placed on these birds, macaws can be nasty and willful, not to mention destructive. In all fairness,

of course, macaws can be precious companions with the charm and affection of the best kitten or puppy. They attach to their owners and require much attention. An ignored macaw will make its discontent known, as its screech is as bad as its bite.

The aforementioned hyacinth macaw is a rare bird that is greatly in demand. There are more accessible members of the genus, such as the familiar blue and gold macaw, the scarlet macaw, and the red and blue macaw.

Lovebirds: Lovebirds derive from Africa principally and generally dwell in the dry savanna regions. These are among the smaller parrots and exhibit short tails. The subtly shaded and brightly colored plumage, a gregarious nature, and the ease of keeping have earned the lovebird a prominent place with bird keepers. Once the birds are properly acclimated, care is simple compared to the keeping of most other parrots. Cages are the most common mode of housing a lovebird, since this diminutive bird comfortably fits into a standard-sized cage. The average lovebird is approximately 12 to 15 centimeters in length. An aviary existence agrees with the lovebird as well, and reproduction is relatively easy to accomplish in captivity. Bird fanciers find the lovebird a fascinating parrot to observe. One of its most unique propensities is the construction of its nest right in the nest box that you provide. It transports twigs and straw for its nest

The varied lorikeet is an attractive, somewhat aggressive bird most frequently kept by experienced fanciers. Properly accommodated, lories make rewarding pets. Photo by L. Robinson.

under its wings.

The largest lovebird, the Abyssinian lovebird (or black-winged lovebird) makes a good cage and aviary bird, but proves less easy to propagate. The Aby is easy to train and gets on well with other birds. The black-masked lovebird has been widely kept for many years in the United States. Their interesting plumage coloration and breeding propensity have found these lovebirds popularity and high acclaim. One of the most accessible of lovebirds is the peach-faced lovebird. Breeding pairs of peach-faced, like most other lovebirds, prove quarrelsome and must be housed separate from other birds to prevent commotion. Certain representatives of the species have convinced keepers that they are a noisy lot. Fischer's lovebirds, like the black-masked lovebirds, are popular and hardy birds. These birds prefer warm ambient temperatures, and require a very dry environment. Since these are easycare, prolific lovebirds, they are highly recommended to the beginning parrot keeper.

For the bird lover who hopes to find the ideal parrot for himself, perhaps visiting a bird show or avian sanctuary in a nearby town would prove helpful. Seeing these remarkable animals live can give a potential owner insights that the written word or photographs cannot.

The peach-fronted lovebird has delighted American and British bird keepers with its regal bearing and pretty face. Lovebirds require less experience to keep than most other parrots. Photo by Michael Gilroy.

Housing

There are several
things to
remember
as far as the housing of parrot-type
birds is concerned. Generally
speaking, the more room a parrot-
type bird, or any other bird for that
matter, can be given, the better. I
much prefer putting a bird on a stand
to confining it in a cage. A stand
gives more freedom of movement to
the bird and allows it more exercise.
It therefore tends to make for a
healthier and happier bird.

A parrot may be tethered to a
stand by means of a small smooth
chain, into which the parrot cannot
bite. The stand should have a
wooden perch and the ends of it
should be capped with metal so that
your parrot cannot chew it to pieces.
Pet shops sell the best stands
available, in a variety of sizes and
styles.

However, for some birds,
especially for young, untamed
parrots, a cage is more practical and
may even be necessary. When a
cage is used, care should be taken
to use one that is not too small. The
bird should have room enough to get
some exercise. A cage that is
sufficient in size for one of the
smaller Amazon parrots would not
be at all adequate for one of the
larger macaws or cockatoos. A guide
to follow in choosing a cage for your
bird is as follows: the cage is too
small if the bird cannot stand in the
center of the middle perch and flap
his wings without touching the bars
of the cage. In other words, the cage
should be considerably wider than
the wing span of the bird that it is to
confine. Parrot-type birds have the
habit of exercising by standing on
the perch and flapping their wings
vigorously. They should be given
every opportunity to do this. Many
cages come with a swing in them. If
this swing interferes with the
exercising of the bird, it should be
taken out. If there are several
perches in the cage, it is better to
have them of different sizes than all
of the same size. This gives your
parrot's feet a rest and change.
Square perches with the corners
rounded off smooth are easier for the
parrot's feet to grip and are not as
tiring as completely round ones.

If you have a metal cage, it may
need a coat of paint occasionally to
prevent corrosion. Care should be
taken to use enamel or some kind of
paint that does not contain lead or
other toxic ingredients. Parrots are
notorious for their habit of chewing
on everything that is within reach.
They will inevitably chew on their
cages from time to time and will get
bits of paint in their mouths. Parrots
are extremely sensitive to lead, and,
if the paint on the cage contains
lead, you may have a very sick or
even a dead bird on your hands. If

you have one of the stainless steel cages, you do not have to worry about painting.

Some people say that a parrot's cage should be enclosed on three sides and should have wire on only one side so that the bird can look in only one direction and there will not be any distractions. This, of course, is ideal during the period when you are training the bird and teaching it to talk, when you do not want the bird's attention drawn away from you by outside influences, but as a general rule, it would be very confining for a bird to be able to look in only one direction. This type of cage does not make for the maximum comfort and happiness of your pet. The most reliable source for the bird's cage is your local pet shop. Among the many supplies and accommodations which the shop sells, cages are a popular commodity, and there is likely a great selection of colors, styles, and sizes from which to choose.

CLEANING

One other very important thing to remember is that the parrot's cage or quarters must be kept clean. In the wild state, the parrot can move about from place to place so that clean quarters are no problem. But in captivity the parrot is completely dependent on its keeper to see that it has clean quarters. Dirty quarters may be a breeding place for parasites and disease.

The cage should be cleaned out at least every other day. It should have a removable tray, which will make for much easier cleaning. This tray should be covered with a piece of paper cut to size, and this in turn should be covered with a generous amount of clean sand or gravel. This will serve a dual purpose. First of all, parrots, like other birds, need sand or gravel to enable them to grind up and digest their food. Secondly, the sand or gravel absorbs the moisture in the droppings and makes conditions more sanitary and cleaning easier.

The food and water dishes should be cleaned out regularly. It is of particular importance that the bird be given fresh water daily. Otherwise there is danger of contamination and disease. In addition to this routine cleaning, the cage should be dismantled and disinfected from time to time. This is a precaution against disease and against mites that may get on your bird (they may be brought in on bird seed) and may breed in the crevices of the cage. A good way to disinfect the cage is to scald the various parts of it with boiling water and a generous amount of a good household disinfectant. After the cage is thoroughly dry, a mite-killing powder, which you can get from your local pet dealer, should be dusted into the crevices of the cage and under the removable tray. The parrot itself should have this powder dusted under its feathers about once a month.

It is not necessary to cover your parrot's cage at night. However, the bird should not be subject to drafts.

OUTDOOR KEEPING

Those parrot owners who live in rural areas may want to construct outdoor pens for the use of their pets in warm weather. This is an excellent way to make sure that your bird gets the proper amount of exercise, fresh air, and sunlight. A shelter should be provided so that the bird can get out of the direct sunlight and out of the rain if it so desires. Many birds enjoy a light shower of warm rain, though.

Some of the parrot-type birds can safely be given their freedom, but this is risky unless you are sure of your bird's tameness and live in a rural area. My father had a macaw that had the freedom of the farm for several years and was quite tame and happy to stay about without being confined. I have also known of double yellow-headed Amazon parrots that were given their freedom and stayed close by. It is a risk to try this unless your bird is tame.

Whatever provision you make for your bird, it is important that you do not confine it where it cannot get out of a direct draft or out of direct sunlight. Parrot-family birds are subject to colds and are likely to catch cold if left in a draft. They may also suffer from sunstroke if unable to get out of the direct sunlight. Either of these may prove to be fatal. The protagonists of the cage with three enclosed sides point out that with such a cage the danger of a direct draft is considerably lessened. However, there are other ways to avoid drafts, and, as we have seen, the general well-being and happiness of your bird dictate against the use of such a cage.

The Alexandrine parakeets must be provided plenty of flying space. A roomy aviary affords these larger birds sufficient exercise area.

Among the Australian parakeets, the blue-winged grass parakeet is reputedly an excellent parent, tending and feeding fledglings beyond their nest-bound days. Photo by L. Robinson.

Feeding

In discussing the feeding of parrot-family birds I believe that the "don'ts" are more important that the "dos." It is important to remember that in the wild state most parrot-family birds are seed eaters and vegetarians. Their digestive systems are not equipped to take care of greasy, fatty foods. Instead of trying to enumerate all of the things that should not be fed to parrots let me simply say that parrots should be confined to the diet set out below. Above all do not feed left-over table scraps and rich greasy foods.

The diet of most of the larger parrot-family birds should consist of equal parts of seeds, green foods, and fruits. The seed part of their diet should be made up of a mixture of sunflower seed, oats, canary seed, and millet. This is the staple seed diet. To this may be added other seeds such as corn, wheat, buckwheat, hemp, and peanuts, and varieties of nuts. They can easily crack the hard shells with their powerful bills. There are exceptions to seed-eating parrots, the lories are a notable example. Vitamins may be added to the seed mixtures in cold weather. About one teaspoonful should be added to a pint of seed and mixed thoroughly before giving it to the bird.

Parrots should have some green foods regularly. Most fresh green garden vegetables are excellent. Most parrots are particularly fond of corn on the cob when it is in the milk stage. The greens should be fed uncooked and unseasoned, of course, but should be washed thoroughly so that any poisonous sprays that have been used may be done away with. About one-third of a parrot's diet should consist of non-citrus fruit, cherries, berries, grapes, apples, etc. Citrus fruit should be fed sparingly, if at all. As an occasional treat, a piece of wholewheat bread, zwieback, or a cracker may be fed.

A piece of cuttle bone should be available to the parrot at all times. This provides the calcium that is necessary for the building of bone, beak, and feathers. Additionally, a supply of sand or gravel should be provided for your bird. This is an absolute necessity. Parrots as well as other birds store sand and gravel in their gizzards and use it to grind their food. They can get along without a fresh supply from which to replenish their store for a short period of time but if deprived of it for any extended period, they will sicken and die.

There are a number of good diet supplements for parrot-type birds on the market. The feeding of a supplement is not absolutely necessary but may help to maintain the health and vigor of your bird, particularly in the winter months.

Training

The ease with which you train your bird to talk or to do tricks depends on the tameness of the bird. Of course, training and taming will depend to a great extent on the intelligence, disposition, and capabilities of the individual bird. To an even greater extent, it will depend on the patience of the trainer. The age of the bird is also an important factor. A young parrot is much easier to train than an old one. The sex of a bird apparently has no bearing on the ease with which it can be tamed or its ability to learn. The females learn just as readily as the males.

The first step in training a parrot is taming it, for you cannot train a wild bird. The younger the bird and the more attention it has had from people, the easier this task will be. If you get a bird that has been hand-raised, you will have no problem taming, but if you get an old bird that has recently been caught or has been neglected, a considerable amount of patience will be required before the bird is tame.

Chances are that you will get neither an extremely young bird nor a fully mature bird. In all probability you will get a young bird that has not had much experience with people and is a bit scared and completely bewildered by its recent changes in environment.

TAMING

To tame your bird you must first of all win its confidence. The bird must know that you do not intend to harm it when you enter the room or approach the cage. A new bird should be allowed to rest and become accustomed to its surroundings for a day or two before any effort is made to tame it.

One of the first steps in taming a bird is to put it in a place where it will have the frequent company of people. In this way, it will become used to human companionship.

After the first day or so, make it a point to be around the cage as much as possible and talk to the bird in quiet and reassuring tones. Do not make any quick movements around the bird; move slowly and deliberately. Place your hands on the cage from time to time, all the while talking to the bird. After a few days, when the bird has become accustomed to this, open the cage door slowly and put your hand inside. Repeat this several times a day for a week or so. Soon your parrot will become accustomed to your hand and will lose its fear of you.

One bit of useful knowledge that is frequently overlooked in the taming of any bird or animal is the power of hunger and the use of food in obtaining the confidence and overcoming the fear that the bird has

Above: The talented Amazon parrot demonstrating its climbing ability. Training devices are available at local pet shops. Blue-fronted Amazon photographed by Isabelle Francais. **Opposite:** A hauntingly beautiful pair of African grey parrots. Due to the species's amitability, tameness, and ability to mimic, many consider this the most desirable of all parrots. Photo by Michael De Freitas.

of mankind. I do not mean that you should starve your bird unnecessarily! But when your bird learns that you are the one to whom it must look for food, it will come to have confidence in you more quickly. If a hungry bird has the choice of eating out of your hand or not at all, it is likely to eat out of your hand. Do not overdo this to the point where you endanger your bird's health or make it paranoid and uncomfortable. In an extremely wild bird, fear is a more powerful drive than hunger.

One of the best ways to use the hunger drive to advantage is to take all food out of the cage or away from the bird after your bird has had its evening feeding. Parrots are in the habit of eating the first thing in the morning, so, with the food unavailable to them until you replace it, they will get pretty hungry. Do not wait too long to replace the food, but

All parrots have the ability to mimic. Certain species show a greater willingness than others. The great-billed parakeet.

when you do so let your hands linger around the feed dish for a few moments. Repeat this procedure for several days and then, some day when you have a little extra time, put the feed dish within your parrot's reach and keep it in your hand. Eventually, depending on how hungry and how afraid it is, your parrot will eat out of the dish that you are holding. Do not make a sudden movement or a loud noise or you will undo all that you have accomplished.

An important thing to remember is that birds kept alone can be tamed more readily than those kept in the presence of other birds. If you are trying to tame more than one bird, you will have more success if you do not keep them in the same cage. It will be even better if they are not even in the same room. If there are other birds present, the bird that you are trying to tame will not become dependent on human companionship but will rely on the other bird or birds for companionship. After the birds are thoroughly tamed and trained, it will not do any harm to keep them together.

TALKING

One of the questions every new parrot owner asks is, "How do I teach my bird to talk?" The answer is simple but again requires patience. You teach your bird to talk by repeating over and over to it what you want it to say. You can start doing this while you are still in the process of taming your bird. In teaching a bird to talk, repeat the word or phrase (it is better to start with a single word, maybe the parrot's name) over and over as often as you can. Say it the first thing in the morning and after the lights are out at night. Repeat it every time you can and soon your bird will reward your patience by repeating it after you. After the bird has mastered the first word, it is the time to start on a new word. The more a bird learns, the more quickly it learns.

Let me pause here to emphasize that it is *not* necessary to split a parrot's tongue to enable it to talk. If anything, this will detract from the parrot's talking ability (not to mention its feeding ability). It certainly will not improve upon the ability of parrot-family birds to mimic the sounds they hear.

During the past few years a number of cassette and compact-disc recordings have reappeared on the market for the purpose of teaching parrots to talk. These recordings can be used very effectively in training parrots and should be played over and over within the bird's hearing. One advantage of using the recording method of teaching is that it can be played repeatedly automatically while you are away or are busy doing something else.

A parrot becomes a member of the family and should, I think, be taught to say the names of members of the family and phrases that have some significance to the family. This is not possible when you teach your

Any parrot must be acclimatized to the human hand. Cockatiel illustration by AnnMarie Freda.

parrot to talk by means of a record unless, of course, you make a record yourself containing family names and significant phrases.

LEARNING TRICKS

The best way to teach a parrot tricks is by rewarding a good performance with praise and a favorite food. Parrots can be taught many of the same tricks that dogs or other animals learn, such as to play dead or to shake hands. When they have been shown what is expected of them, they should be rewarded for a good performance.

Health

There are several things that you should know if the health, happiness, and general well-being of your bird are to be maintained. First of all is the matter of feeding. Remember that parrots are vegetarians. Their digestive systems are designed to take care of seeds, fruits, and greens and not greasy or fatty foods. More pet parrots are "killed with kindness," i.e., by feeding table scraps, than from any other cause. A parrot may get by for a time on such unwholesome fare but eventually it will sicken and unless it is put on a good diet will probably die.

Another very important thing to remember is that your bird should be kept in a comfortable place. The cage or stand should not be placed in a direct draft. Parrots and their kin are quite susceptible to colds and, if left in a position where they cannot get out of a draft, they will almost inevitably catch cold. In a short period of time, a cold can go from bad to worse and may be fatal. There are some antibiotic remedies on the market that may be given to your bird to combat a cold, but, if your bird develops a bad cold in spite of your efforts, I would strongly advise that a veterinarian be consulted. The doctor will have some specific remedy that will prove more effective than your home remedies.

Care should be taken also not to place your parrot so that it cannot get out of direct sunlight. Parrots are subject to sunstroke and may fall victim to the direct rays of the sun if they are so situated that they cannot get out of them. Sunstroke may be fatal.

Again, never underestimate the importance of cleanliness in the bird's living quarters.

BATHS

A question often asked by the new parrot owner is "Do parrots bathe?" This question is impossible to answer with a simple "yes" or "no." Some parrots will bathe in a shallow dish of water; others will not. At any rate for the first few weeks that you have your parrot he should be given the opportunity to bathe. A shallow dish that is not too light or too slippery should be provided for your parrot to bathe in. Ideal for this purpose is an earthenware saucer that is made to set a large flower pot in. These saucers are about the right depth, are heavy enough so that they are not easily upset, and have a rough surface so that the parrot is not likely to slip.

If, after a reasonable trial period, you find that your bird will not bathe, you should spray your bird with a fine mist of water. This may be done by putting lukewarm water into an insect spray gun and spraying it directly on

Spectacular and elegant, the cockatoo provides amusement and affection on sunny and rainy days. The great white or umbrella cockatoo is a highly favored parrot. Photo by T. Tilford.

your bird; an atomizer or a plastic spray bottle may also be used for this purpose. This should be done at least every other day.

The natural habitat of many parrots is the tropical rain forests. In these forests it rains practically every day, and the rain comes down through the trees to the parrots as a warm mist which thoroughly wets their feathers. This is the only bath they take. You can duplicate this condition by use of your spray gun.

MITES

Remember that it is a wise precaution to obtain a good mite powder made especially for parrots and other cage birds. There are a number of such powders on the market. About once a month both the parrot and its living quarters should be dusted liberally with this powder. The bird should have the powder blown up under its feathers and should be dusted all over. This is just as a precaution. If any mites should happen to come in, they can be headed off before they get a good start by this periodic dusting.

If you should happen to discover that mites are present on your bird, just follow the directions on the container that your mite powder comes in. You should also disinfect the cage with boiling water. If you keep your bird's quarters clean and dust both quarters and bird periodically, you will not have to worry about mites. Any infestation that may occur will be nipped in the bud.

FIRST AID

One thing that is of prime importance to remember is that if your parrot does get sick for any reason whatsoever, the first precaution is to keep it warm. The body temperature of birds is higher than that of many other animals and when they are sick and run-down a thorough chilling can be disastrous. If possible raise the temperature to 85°F or 90°F for a sick bird. This may be made possible by putting the bird into a box in which has been placed a large light bulb. The bulb will give off enough heat to keep the box warm. The bulb may be covered with wire and covered with a flame-resistant cloth to prevent the sick bird from burning itself and to keep the intense light from making it uncomfortable.

Pet supply companies offer hospital cages that are equipped with heating units, thermometers, and thermostats. These cages are, of course, ideal for keeping a sick bird warm and are reasonably inexpensive.

GENERAL TIPS

People from time to time ask about clipping the wing feathers of a parrot so that he cannot fly. Many experts advise against this. If your bird is confined to a cage or a stand, there is no absolute necessity for it. If you set your bird at liberty, it would be extremely dangerous to render it unable to fly. Flight is the only means of escape that a bird has from a dog, cat, or other natural enemy. If deprived of that, it is defenseless against any approaching predator.

The most essential thing for maintaining the happiness and general well-being of your parrot is that you give it the attention it requires. Any bird or animal, if it is to be a good pet, requires a certain amount of attention. This is an absolute essential. Without it a parrot, deprived of both the companionship of other birds and human attention, will soon grow dull, unresponsive, and sullen.

A neglected bird often turns to feather plucking, a disfiguring habit that is extremely hard to break.

On the other hand, if your bird receives adequate attention, it will be a most rewarding and amusing pet. I do not mean that you must devote any inordinate amount of time to your parrot, but you should spend a little while talking to it and playing with it every day if possible. Generally speaking, the more attention you give to any pet the more rewarding that pet is. This is certainly true of parrot-family birds.

In conclusion, let me caution the prospective parrot purchaser to be sure to get a good bird. In parrots, as in everything else, you get what you pay for. A young, partially tamed bird will cost more than an old one but will be easier to tame and a more satisfying pet in the long run. Get your bird from a reputable pet dealer and you can be sure of getting a nice pet. You will run a risk if you try to save money and get a cheap bird from a second-rate dealer.

Bibliography

PARROTS OF THE WORLD
By Joseph M. Forshaw
ISBN 0-87666-959-3
TFH P-753
Hard cover, 584 pages, 9½ x 12½
Almost 300 large color plates depicting
close to 500 different parrots; many line
illustrations.

THE WORLD OF LOVEBIRDS
By J. Brockmann & W. Lantermann
ISBN 0-86622-927-2
H-1092
Hardcover, 6 x 9", 192 pages,
71 full-color photos.

ENCYCLOPEDIA OF AMAZON PARROTS
By Klaus Bosch & Ursula Wedde
ISBN 0-86622-797-0
TFH H-1055
Hard cover, 8½ x 11", 128 pages
Illustrated with full-color photos and range
maps.

HANDBOOK OF COCKATOOS
By Dr. A.E. Decoteau
ISBN 0-86622-798-9
TFH H-1030
Hard cover, 5½ x 8", 160 pages
Highly illustrated, contains many full-color
photos.

THE GREY PARROT
By Wolfgang de Grahl
ISBN 0-86622 094-1
TFH H-1088
Hardcover, 6 x 9", 224 pages
80 full-color and black and white photos.

THE ENCYCLOPEDIA OF COCKATIELS
By George A. Smith
ISBN 0-87666-958-5
TFH PS-743
Hardcover, 5 ½ x 8", 256 pp.
60 full-color photos, 108 black and white
photos.

Distributed in the UNITED STATES by T.F.H. Publications, Inc., One
T.F.H. Plaza, Neptune City, NJ 07753; in CANADA to the Pet Trade
by H & L Pet Supplies Inc., 27 Kingston Crescent, Kitchener, Ontario
N2B 2T6; Rolf C. Hagen Ltd., 3225 Sartelon Street, Montreal 382
Quebec; in CANADA to the Book Trade by Macmillan of Canada (A
Division of Canada Publishing Corporation), 164 Commander
Boulevard, Agincourt, Ontario M1S 3C7; in ENGLAND by T.F.H.
Publications, P.O. Box 15 Waterlooville PO7 6BQ; in AUSTRALIA
AND THE SOUTH PACIFIC by T.F.H. (Australia) Pty. Ltd., Box 149,
Brookvale 2100 N.S.W., Australia; in NEW ZEALAND by Ross
Haines & Son, Ltd., 82 D Elizabeth Knox Place, Panmure, Auckland,
New Zealand; in the PHILIPPINES by Bio-Research, 5 Lippay Street,
San Lorenzo Village, Makati, Rizal; in SOUTH AFRICA by Multipet
Pty. Ltd., P.O. Box 35347, Northway, 4065, South Africa. Published
by T.F.H. Publications, Inc. Manufactured in the United States of
America by T.F.H. Publications, Inc.

Everything you need to know to start right with
Parrots

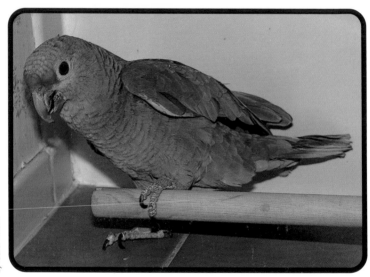

Front cover photo by Fred Harris. Back cover photo by Carol Thiem.

t.f.h.
YF-113

ISBN 0-86622-070-4

90000

9 780866 220705

0 18214 20704 7

T.F.H. PUBLICATIONS, INC. • 1 T.F.H. Plaza • Third & Union Aves. • Neptune, NJ 07753

99-21